W9-BJR-375

DATE DUE

Neighborhood Walk

Small Town

Peggy Pancella

Heinemann Library
Chicago, Illinois

© 2006 Heinemann Library
a division of Reed Elsevier Inc.
Chicago, Illinois

Customer Service   888–454–2279

Visit our website at www.heinemannlibrary.com

Photo research by Jill Birschbach
Designed by Joanna Hinton-Malivoire and Q2A Creative
Printed in China by South China Printing Co.

10 09 08 07 06
10 9 8 7 6 5 4 3 2

Library of Congress Cataloging-in-Publication Data
Pancella, Peggy.
   Small town / Peggy Pancella.
      p. cm. -- (Neighborhood walk)
   Includes bibliographical references and index.
   ISBN 1-4034-6218-6 (hc) -- ISBN 1-4034-6224-0 (pb)
   1. Cities and towns--Juvenile literature. 2. City and town life--Juvenile
literature. I. Title. II. Series.
   HT152.P38 2006
   307.76--dc22
                              2005010761

Acknowledgments
The author and publisher are grateful to the following for permission to reproduce copyright material: Corbis pp. **4** (bottom), **5** (top, Royalty-Free), **14**, **16** (Neil Beckerman), **25**; Getty Images pp. **10** (PhotoDisc), **11** (SW Productions/Brand X Pictures); Heinemann Library pp. **4** (top, Robert Lifson), **5** (bottom, Rudi Von Briel), **6** (Scott Braut), **7** (Scott Braut), **8** (Scott Braut), **9** (Scott Braut), **12** (Scott Braut), **15** (Scott Braut), **17** (Scott Braut), **18** (Scott Braut), **19** (Jill Birschbach), **20** (Brian Warling), **21** (Brian Warling), **22** (Scott Braut), **23** (Scott Braut), **24** (Scott Braut), **26** (Scott Braut), **29** (Robert Hashimoto); Photo Edit, Inc. **13** (Mark Richards), **27** (Jeff Greenberg), **28** (David Young-Wolff)

Cover photograph reproduced with the permission of Getty Images (Stone/Peter Pearson)

Some words are shown in bold, **like this**. You can find out what they mean by looking in the glossary.

Contents

Let's Visit a Small Town 4

Homes 6

Getting Around 8

Schools 10

Working 12

Keeping Safe 14

Shopping 16

Food 18

Libraries 20

Money and Mail 22

Other Places in a Small Town 24

Having Fun 26

The Town Comes Together 28

Glossary 30

More Books to Read 31

Index 32

Let's Visit a Small Town

People everywhere live in **neighborhoods**. A neighborhood is a small part of a larger **community**, such as a city or town. A neighborhood's people and places help to make it special.

4

Some neighborhoods are parts of small towns. A town is a small community that is not part of a city or its **suburbs**. There are usually very few large buildings in a small town.

Homes

Most people in small towns live in houses. Some houses are large, and others are small. Many houses have yards where people can play and relax. The homes nearby each other make up a **neighborhood**.

Some neighborhoods have many large houses.

These houses are connected to each other.

Some people live in joined homes called **town houses**. Others live in apartments above stores in the center of town. These homes often do not have large yards. People may play in neighborhood parks instead.

Getting Around

The center of town is sometimes called the **business district**.

A small town usually has one or two main streets. Most homes and businesses are near these roads. People sometimes drive cars to get from place to place in the town.

People may also walk or ride bikes to get around. They do not have to go far because places are so close together. For this reason, small towns do not usually offer **public transportation** like cities do.

It is easy to get from place to place on a bike.

Schools

Small towns have few people, so they need few schools. A town may have only one grade school and one high school. A very small town may share a school with a neighboring town.

Buses may pick up children who do not live near the school.

Town schools may have grassy fields or playgrounds.

School buildings in towns are not usually very large. Many have play areas nearby. Some of the students walk or ride bikes to get to school. Others ride in cars or on school buses.

Working

Many people work in the town where they live. There is usually a **business district** in the center of town. People from the town own and work at shops, restaurants, and other businesses there.

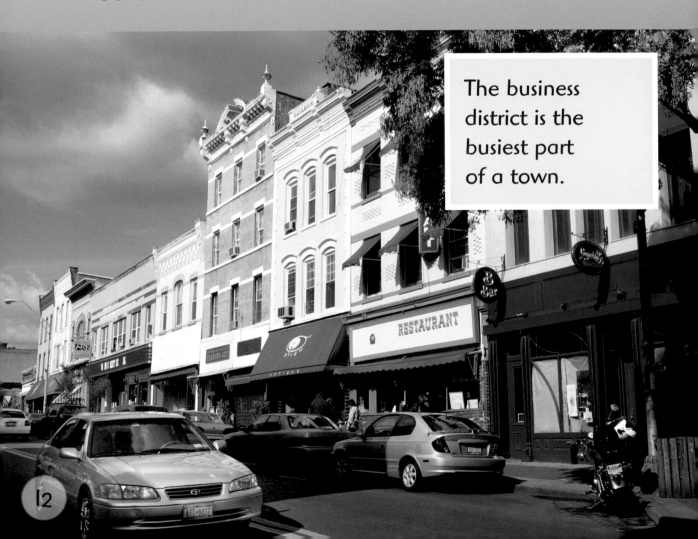

The business district is the busiest part of a town.

Factories are places where there are machines to make large amounts of goods.

Some workers build and repair the roads and buildings that the town needs. Other people work outside the town. They may work at factories, farms, or other kinds of businesses. Some workers even **commute** to jobs in the nearest city.

Keeping Safe

Many workers help keep the town safe. Most small towns have at least a few police officers. The police get to know people so they can help when problems happen.

Police **patrol** the town in cars or on foot.

Emergency workers take good care of their vehicles so they are always ready to help.

Some towns have firefighters and **emergency** workers, too. These workers rush to help when people are hurt, sick, or in danger. Workers from nearby towns sometimes come to help when they are needed.

Shopping

In a town's **business district**, there are many small shops and restaurants along the main road. People can walk from place to place to buy what they need. These shops usually close at night.

Stores in towns sell many different items.

Larger stores may be found close to the town.

There are sometimes other shopping areas outside of towns. Large supermarkets, **department stores**, and **strip malls** sell many kinds of products. People can buy everything they need in just one stop.

Food

Farmers' markets sell fresh fruits and vegetables.

People in small towns can buy food in different places. Some shop at grocery stores in town. Others go to larger supermarkets outside the town. Many people also grow fruits and vegetables or buy them at **farmers' markets**.

A town usually has a few small restaurants where people can eat. Towns near large highways sometimes have restaurants or **truck stops** near the **exit ramp**. People who are traveling can stop there for a meal.

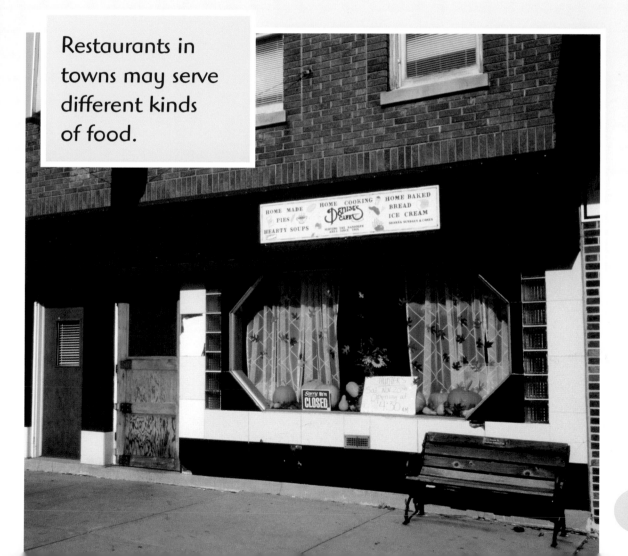

Restaurants in towns may serve different kinds of food.

Libraries

Many towns have libraries. There is usually only one library in a small town. People can borrow books and look up information. There may be computers to use or special activities to do, too.

Some libraries have special areas for children.

Librarians help people find and check out books.

Town libraries often do not have very many books. Sometimes **librarians** can order new books. They may borrow books from libraries in other towns. Librarians can also use computers to find out information that people need.

Money and Mail

Most small towns have two or more banks to handle people's money. These are usually in the **business district**. Some banks also have drive-up windows and **ATMs** for people to use.

ATMs make banking quick and easy.

Letter carriers may walk or drive to deliver the mail.

A small town has a post office, too. People can mail letters and packages here. Once the mail is sorted, letter carriers bring it to homes and businesses.

Other Places in a Small Town

Towns have many other important buildings. In the **town hall**, **government** leaders make plans and rules for the town. There may also be churches, temples, and other places of worship.

A church is often one of a town's tallest buildings.

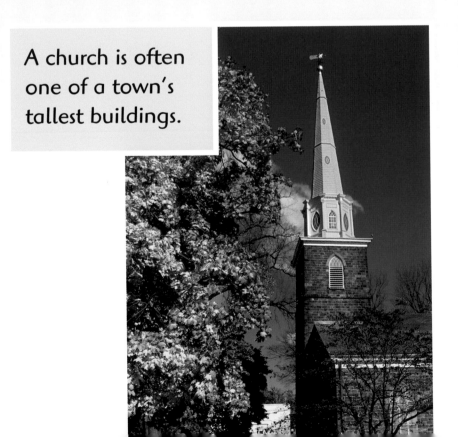

Hospitals help people who need immediate care.

Towns have doctors' offices where people who are sick or hurt can go for help. Many small towns do not have hospitals, though. People who need a hospital may have to drive to a city or larger town.

Having Fun

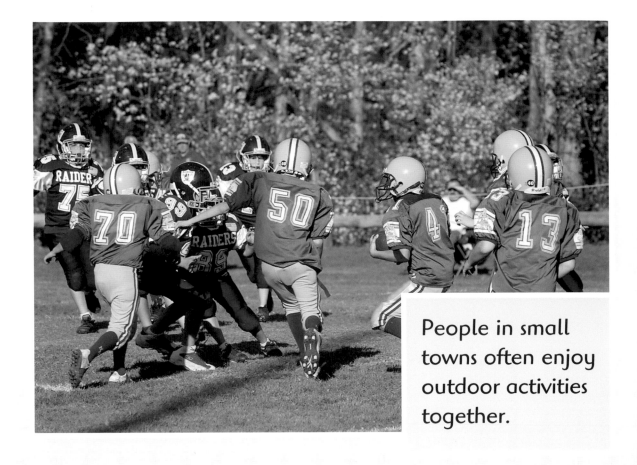

People in small towns often enjoy outdoor activities together.

Many people in small towns like to play or relax in their own yards. Most towns also have parks, ball fields, and other places for outdoor activities. People enjoy hiking, fishing, playing sports, and having picnics and cookouts.

Many small towns have theaters where people can watch movies or hear music concerts. There may be a **museum** that teaches about the town's history. People sometimes travel to the city for special activities, too.

Musicians sometimes play music in the park.

The Town Comes Together

People may help to keep their town clean.

Because towns are small, many people know each other. They work together for the good of their **community**. They may collect food and clothing or do special activities to raise money for those in need.

People in towns gather to have fun, too. There may be parades or fairs at special times. People share food, music, games, and fun. All these things make small towns great places to live.

There are lots of fun things to do at a fair.

Glossary

ATM bank machine that people use to put in and take out money

business district area in the middle of a town where there are many businesses

community group of people who live in one area, or the area where they live

commute travel from home to work and back

department store large store that sells many different kinds of things

emergency sudden event that makes you act quickly

exit ramp road that leads off a highway to a smaller road

farmers' market place where people sell things that were grown or made on farms

government people who make rules for a community, or the rules they make

librarian person who works in a library

museum place where special or important items are shown

neighborhood small area of a city or town

patrol travel through an area to keep it safe

public transportation ways of travel that are organized and that everyone can use

strip mall   one long building divided into many different stores

suburb   community that is just outside a city

town hall   building where the leaders of a town meet

town house   house that is joined to the houses next to it, usually in a row

truck stop   place where drivers can stop to get food, fuel, and rest

More Books to Read

Caseley, Judith. *On the Town: A Community Adventure.* New York: Greenwillow, 2002.

Kalman, Bobbie. *What Is a Community?: from A to Z.* New York: Crabtree Publishing, 2000.

Kehoe, Stasia Ward. *I Live in a Town.* New York: PowerKids Press, 1999.

Turnbauer, Lisa. *Living in a Small Town.* Mankato, Minn.: Capstone Press, 2005.

Index

banks 22
business district 8,
    12-13, 16, 22

churches and temples
    24
cities 4-5, 9, 13, 25, 27

emergency workers 15

firefighters 15
food 18-19, 28-29

government 24

homes 6-8, 23
hospitals 25

libraries 20-21

museums 27

neighborhoods 4-5,
    6-7

parks and play areas
    6-7, 26
police 14
post offices 23

restaurants 12, 16, 19

schools 10-11
sports 26-27
stores 12, 16-18

theaters 27
transportation 8-11,
    13

work 12-13